ON THE SHORES OF WELCOME HOME

ON THE SHORES OF WELCOME HOME

POEMS

BRUCE WEIGL

AMERICAN POETS CONTINUUM SERIES, NO. 175

BOA EDITIONS, LTD. ❦ ROCHESTER, NY ❦ 2019

Manufactured in the United States of America

First Edition
19 20 21 22 7 6 5 4 3 2 1

Publications by BOA Editions, Ltd.—a not-for-profit corporation under section 501 (c) (3) of the United States Internal Revenue Code—are made possible with funds from a variety of sources, including public funds from the Literature Program of the National Endowment for the Arts; the New York State Council on the Arts, a state agency; and the County of Monroe, NY. Private funding sources include the Max and Marian Farash Charitable Foundation; the Mary S. Mulligan Charitable Trust; the Rochester Area Community Foundation; the Ames-Amzalak Memorial Trust in memory of Henry Ames, Semon Amzalak, and Dan Amzalak; the LGBT Fund of Greater Rochester; and contributions from many individuals nationwide. See Colophon on page 100 for special individual acknowledgments.

Cover Design: Sandy Knight
Interior Design and Composition: Richard Foerster
BOA Logo: Mirko

Library of Congress Cataloging-in-Publication Data

Names: Weigl, Bruce, 1949– , author.
Title: The shores of welcome home : poems / Bruce Weigl.
Description: First edition. | Rochester, NY : BOA Editions, Ltd., 2019. |
Series: American poets continuum series ; no. 175
Identifiers: LCCN 2019019107 | ISBN 9781942683896 (pbk.)
Subjects: LCSH: Vietnam War, 1961–1975—Psychological aspects—Poetry. | Veterans—Mental health—United States—Poetry. | Older veterans—United States—Poetry. | War poetry, American.
Classification: LCC PS3573.E3835 A6 2019 | DDC 811/.54—dc23 LC record available at https://lccn.loc.gov/2019019107

BOA Editions, Ltd.
250 North Goodman Street, Suite 306
Rochester, NY 14607
www.boaeditions.org
A. Poulin, Jr., Founder (1938–1996)

For Sonny Bunzo and Mila Vy

Contents

Part One

Part Two

Part Three

Our schemes are so fragile a fire
begins mincing childishly through
the backstreets, through our fingers
and we'll never forget;
the whole world is a library of fire
and we'll never get out of it . . .

—James Tate

Against Forgetting (Two)

I didn't remember where to start my life.
If you could translate the screams of brain cells
under duress
it would be deafening,
like a waterfall of nails down the blackboard.
I thought of this in the fourth grade.
I figured out that words meant exactly what they said,
and at the same time
meant nothing at all. School
was downhill for me
from then on

Part One

The Elephant Gift in the Room

Sun refuses the last nanosecond before night;
stars explode in your cold head—old, nostalgic bombs and rockets,
    classic mortar rounds—
but no one understands, and no one hears you speak, and no one
    even sees you
standing there in your sixty-two years, soldier.

You Can Hide

You can hide behind this
You can hide behind my eyes
You can hide behind the trigger
You can be hurled unnamed through dusty sunlight
And not know anything because a rocket even close
Will do that to you

Go away slim shadows
Open as if in communion but nothing goes away
I walked and I crawled
The ocean crossed me
Asleep in my cocoon but nothing goes away
Waiting like it does always
Something that gets ahead of you somehow
As in an ambush a beautiful word
On the mouth to say.

Painted Box Buried in the Yard

The yard of our sadness where we buried
things after some man hung himself in the
basement of our apartment. Circa five years old
who found him was named me, but the I didn't
know drunk and fucking around from hung
right off to death and it was a long time before
I put that particular two and two
together, and saw him in my mind's movie
more than once, swinging there, pale as our autumn
sky. Sometimes you need a great notion to
survive even one single moment
of your life; someone pushed to the
edge, and then see what happens.

Grace Being Saved

Grace being saved, even between thunder raps
under the storm a certain light
bends itself through clouds and around trees
and you can find it there lighting up
like a catastrophe then gone
as a kiss, never to come back.

Or there's my other face in the mirror
in the Ascending Dragon Hotel, Tống Đản
Street, though I don't know who he is,
nor do I remember such elegance, but what
you see in the mirror is nothing, and is not
nothing, the way time wanted me that day;
the way time came with its voracious, drooling
jaws and snatched the light away.

Anecdote of the Impresario of My Brain

The dead people I see are not happy when they know that I see
    them. They frown a strange death mask at me from passing
    motorcars, or in the dimly-lit
hallways of unfamiliar buildings like the one where the keeper of
    records presides.
He knows everything about us, but he doesn't know that he is dead.
    When I ask for my records, he refuses to look at me so that
    the darkness gathered in the corners
begins to reel outward, exactly like a tiny tornado.
If you've seen that then you know what the fuck I'm talking about,
    climbing the ladder,
and the rigmarole of other places where the sidewalks are poured in
    a different paradigm
than ours, and the rivers are not interrogated about their direction
    so flow the bright waters
straight through you is how it feels later on, back in custody.

Some Stages of the Mayfly

You don't have to write anything down; you don't
have to say anything at all or even
gesture with your head or your body or
your face or your eyes or your hands. You don't
have to make a sound and still someone will
understand you the way a mayfly
understands at a precisely particular
angle of light that it's time to emerge
from the nymph and swim towards the light and
towards great wings that burst through to dry on the
gleaming surface, then carry them off
into dark trees from which they parachute
on thin wings that same night to die.

Against Poetry

I didn't want to hurt the earth
so when I weeded the garden
I spoke to the plants like souls
the way the teacher taught me

and never mind the centuries of suffering
the razor sting of words
that won't mean anything
except to tell one doom or another
and not even your own. The night
delivered to the stars
matters; the distance the light must travel
painfully long but coming for you.

River of Blood in One Man

Dressing up for your guests for example,
    the blood so red when it comes from where it's not.
        So red on the paper, and so much

that you stand up, fixing your trousers, and walk
    out into the formality of nothing
        but life and death encounters with strangers,

and weirdness in your correspondence too;
    please, let me have my iron mask; the blood
        that's crimson's not as bad as the darker

red that comes from deep inside, river that it is,
    beautiful meanness of the heart that keeps beating,
        empty in its cage of love.

Prayer for My Teacher

A sky in my head tonight,
only I don't know if it's a star
or not, I don't know what
it wants, like the wind surely
must want something the way
it calls me through the trees
and across the still green lawns
of my quiet neighbors like someone
hissing a curse or a last
blessing before hell, but what
I found inside the dark
this time was a wave of something
warm that almost seemed to,
or did, hold me there
for a long enough second
so I could see the brightly
sonic outline of everything
that wasn't there, and be freed
by that and made happy for you,

so here is the smile of my mouth,
only half, as it should be, and here
is the smile of my eyes I hope
you see some light in, and here
is the smile of my fingers held up
in the shape of the lotus, that heals
and that satisfies,
but I don't know why peace
is still too much to ask for,
or why the landscape must
include the inconsequential
corpses from both sides,
as if posed for some demonic
puppet show for the generals

and their overweight children
to enjoy in the imperial garden.
The flaws of our reason have finally
shivered into shifting plates
of what we knew all along,
come to pass.

Against Forgetting (One)

Startling when the brain can see the mind, accomplished
only with the most precise surgery, for example,
performed by beings whose hands are made of a kind
of glass that you are not allowed to touch.
You are not allowed to ask certain questions afterwards;
questions about the paradigm are especially discouraged,
and never appreciated. They maintain security at all times.
I want to ask if I am the same, or different,

but it is not allowed, and even before
the thought completes itself and the words are not yet
on my lips, someone is tsking to me inside of my head,
wagging their finger like a mother or a drug cop in the rearview
mirror of my horizon. One misstep
in this situation could bring trouble, ask just about any

dead soul still spinning around in circles,
wondering, What the fuck was that?

Fragments in Translation from the Vietnamese

The presence of natives is beneficial
to our overall splendor,
whenever that happens.

Someone is waiting under a dim light in a dark room;
he is not difficult to reach,
or as far away as he seems.

Do not touch the teacher.
Leave the temple fragments alone.
Make a Buddha with three stones.

You will look through an alleyway
that appears in the jungle
and seems to go on and on,

your glass shoes slipping
as you try to keep up.

Yet who wants to remember all of the dead
is important
to the dead.

You think you feel the world
inside of you,
a soaking rain on the bamboo roof
that mimics the sound of loss.

Lotus

There is a certain slant of light
just at the rising of the sun
above the lake that cuts across
the lotus and wakes slowly the blossoms until
the blossoms become the lake like a white
and green jungle.
                                    Sometimes it is impossible
to move. Love is like that, the way
the beauty makes it impossible
even to breathe, drowning
in the heartbreak
of blossoms, tangled in the roots
of a thing that can't be.

Reading the River

Death plus limestone river
equals swirling dervish currents
night bank   grass wings
just inside of this world
breath   you could say

Ode to Cabeza de Vaca

What good is it to see for miles and miles,
the tired, lonely explorer said to the fat queen,
prostrate by her feet, still not allowed to go home.
I am dying of omens that no one recognizes
or understands, and I am under anesthesia
again, veil over my brain, so I may
be wrong or confused about even simple things.
It's not what you think, the other side, not a dream
or a movie, but more a sifting diamond sand
washed up with the bodies on the shore of every
welcome home so don't tread there; don't be anything at all.

A Late Corrupted Flash

I couldn't think of anything to do;
I was out among the traffic in the street,
but didn't make my way, my view
was blocked, and nothing left but new defeats,

and then I stepped into a line of trees
I know I'd seen before, the sulfur smell,
the bullets whizzing past like wild bees.
I wasn't where I thought I was. I fell

again, through something damp, like air, then back
inside the traffic jam I knew was caused
by me, my drifting as I do, my lack
of self-control, to know just when to pause

before I cross into that other place
that somehow always stays inside my soul.
I wish that I could say a simple grace
would be enough to make me whole,

but I was lost inside the river so I
didn't move, and thought I'd wait it out,
the night, in all its splendor, the lies
that let me stand there, as if without a doubt.

In the morning someone came, or no one came at all.
I knew somehow, I'd wake and be alive,
but never be the same again, a fall
from grace so hard and fast, I can't aide.

That night I died, and it was not like dreaming
although my heart kept beating, my brain a whir.
The world outside my mind stopped meaning
anything at all, so you can't see me through the blur

of monumental metaphors the doctors rig
like precious metal crosses
that hang a name around my latest jig,
no peace, and never mind the other losses.

Not My Brain Talkin'

This is not my brain talking. This is a brain with a shunt talking
    and trying to write something down. I thought there was a
    music in
the words, no matter how you laid them out across the page; across
    your arm the needle runs pink tracks to red. If I love you I
    would
cook your medicine, melt the pills the doctors dole. I would sweetly
    tie the rubber hose to swell the vein with
blood. I would do it all
and love you even more, and all the things that can go wrong with
    promises
is the name of this matinée,
but I'm here for the duration and nobody gets left behind.

WORDS FOR MY PAL WHO IS DEAD

Someone hands me a cell phone in the soupy dark and somehow, I
know that the phone's been rigged to allow me to speak to the
dead,
and you are the first one I call.
Your voice is the same only lighter and unconnected to
the things of this poor world, yet I could feel the weight of
you
through space, the body you had been but are no more. I could see
the spirit of you, spiraling out of the phone like smoke from a
cigarette, in the cold.
So, what the hell was that to come into my sleep, and then just
leave? We fish different waters now is all.

The Long-Term Consequences of the Convoy Leading to Pegasus in the Fallen World

Or when I packed myself up for the loony bin
I didn't know it was the loony bin at the time
was my lousy problem and I blame myself
for that and I ended up in a field I know
is littered with mines because I've seen it before
beside a river named Cà Lu if my brain allows
me just one memory one sane moment like the one
the photon bright flashes the doctors held inches from
my face brought back a radiant time that no one in
the room could know but me like the field of mines
I had stood next to on the LZ, and walked around
more than once and watched a parachute of something
drift off target and land there almost softly the lights
the doctors flashed in my eyes and the saline they pumped
into my veins and the thirty hours without sleep
brought that morning right back into the room and that
morning became the day of the longest night of
the seven dead in a single bunker from artillery
fired across an invisible line in the dark night of small
arms fire along the river and movement in the
high grass voices radio noise sometimes even their music
night of the separation of my soul from my body
such a violent tearing I couldn't even feel.

The World Part II

Dogwood blossoms fill
the air like snow and dust
the branches of the trees
and you have to close your eyes
to see the luminous shapes
and forms and don't say Save me
to just any god.
We used to have a compass
in our heads when the sun
did not reach through the triple
canopy and at night no stars.
Still, your body feels
where the river is,
where the crossroads disappear
into walls of green bamboo.
Now, I don't know where I am,
or why I brought you here
or what I had in mind,
but I'll give you my hand to take.
I'll reach through this unfolding.

The Unbearable Weight of a Friend

In translation I would say
I sit on top of the dresser.
The rice is not quite ready to harvest.
The river changes direction
like our flag in the wind.
Everything changes
continuously like the sky,
except my heart
stays the same dark
on the beach of an island;
I don't know if I died there
but I know I am nothing without you,
and that in certain light
we share a life together,
unimaginable as skin on skin.

Act of Contrition

Plaintive birdsong
does not ease my brain

from its spinning

ache that won't allow me to live
except for birds.

I call my backyard a flyway.
Through time I watch them beat

and hear them even in my sleep
call out to each of us

something more human
than you might expect.

It isn't god that I'm thinking about
but something like a god.

Altarpiece of the Misericordia

One man's face is completely
without features; another
wears a black hood over his
face, his body hunched away.
Eight others pray under the
wings of the solemn, holy
mother of god, yet it's an
atmospheric light that pulls

you deep inside the misery;
it's what the painter didn't paint
that lets you see what kind of
light that suffering can be,
the white hot burning up of
everything you thought you could
believe, holy father, son, and ghost.

Lotus, West Lake, 2010

The lotus has spread so far and are so thick
in the southern shallows of the lake
that it's impossible for the small round boat
the lotus gatherer paddles to move any further
so, she is frozen there as on a Chinese vase.
I am watching this in what feels like a dream
that won't let me wake up. She paddles, barely moving,
and below the surface she slices through the stems,
so soon her boat is filled and overflowing. I am watching this
through an evening mist that shimmers in my memory.
And then she's gone, but not the way the light is gone,
and more the way the darkness comes to take its place.
I thought the light was everlasting.
I thought she would come for the lotus again and again,
but things end; things fall apart from their luminous insides,
and she disappeared into the exact center of the sun
going down hard and slow beyond the lake.

Before it's light, I'm in my bed awake,
I hear the women calling out the names
of what they sell, before the traffic noise
will drown them out. *Hoa sen* a voice calls out,
but only once then lost
inside a world that isn't there.

The Hà Nội Winds Bringing Winter to the Old-World Elegy

The soon to be bare winter branches
don't exactly tremble—that's a human thing—
but they move in the wind of my waiting
in what looks like the shiver that love brings
to your neurons, right down to the cells
who are happy for some company, after all.
I could sit out here all day and watch the world
leave us behind, and not have a single regret
except for not living even harder and faster
than I did, giving up to immutable green space
my body, and then later, my soul down by the river
whose name I may not utter, please
don't make me tell you what happened there, the bare
branches are enough in their trembling like a shiver
to say all that needs to be said. The room I'm in
is getting smaller, with every faded moment's life,
and we know what that means. Your heart may beat
in time with the umbrella's flapping in patio wind,
but it doesn't mean you belong anywhere;
it doesn't mean you're connected to anything that could save you
or pull you back into the flock of care we imagine. No.

The Ineffable as Sad

You want to be sad?
I'll show you something
sad: the woman loved the man
so much
even under foreign
skies that she memorized
his long list of pills
for the dying, and set them
in his open hand
in the morning
and at every night.

Part Two

On the Shores of Welcome Home

I

I want to sing an old man's song,
the evening's blue gray light just gone.
I want to find the immorality
of our disinterest;
it's our business
to know the geography
of the countries
we bring misery.

First there is the flesh
or the fleshy insides of
a thing or two
coming to the surface
in the flooded backyards; brother
do you know how it feels
not to have
enough food or water
for even your own angels
who float above the trailer park's
cold descent,
what it means to sleep
in bone numbing pain
that comes from living a bottomless life
where even death cannot be afforded,
so far beyond a blue relief?

*

The moral center's out of whack.
It may not find
its own way back
so the befuddled torturer
imagines his late dinner,
and the flesh of a single fat white larva

is sucked down the throat of a starving
man. Don't be befuddled too. Don't
pretend there's nothing to believe in
like a cascade of flowers
thrown into the mass graves
to try and bear the smell away.
Pitch. Ash. Sand of bones
release me.
I shiver in my hot bed
at the mention of your name.

*

During moments of mortal fear and terror
in the kingdom of needs
a clarity moves across your landscape
so that suddenly everything appears bright,
and in a stupor of amazement you see
what had been there all along.
But don't mourn on me,
mourn on your own selves.

Flesh of chaos. Flesh of green jungle,
rapid eye movement, rockets, mortar rounds,
voices from the bush at night, crippling,
antagonistic fear
reeling outward through the years
like a sharp wire. Sometimes there's
not even time to die. Trip flare light
trapped on the rain beyond all reason.

*

Like a virus, you can bring another country
home with you and not even know.
A country can take you so far away, you will never come back.
        Brother
can you spare me a rhyme? There used to be a greater kindness;
there used to be a thing you could feel inside that binds us,

the holy sameness that we are.
Flesh of men who sit on thrones
and spend the lives of others like dollars. Night
is not safe anymore,
and the violated name our times.
Flesh of the savior, not in the host.
Flesh of the ones who took with their hands
what they had no right to own.

II

They sell rivets that fail. They own companies
that reap, after a cheap sowing of the young and the helpless,
a great pile of money so high you could never spend it all.
At the bottom of this hill
people pick through a garbage pit for pieces of fruit or bread.
You can't ask
Why don't you care or
Why don't you help?
of the people who own the war
the way people own a Coca Cola plant
or a car dealership; they will look at you
like you don't understand and turn back
to their conversations with minor officials.

III

Some cops kill. No big deal. They don't know how we feel,
how even when our hearts are shredded like lace
there's no place we can hide.
I don't care what you say; I don't hear what you pray;
it's just your own dismay at the dying gods
and the churches turned to malls,
and the long and hard fall
through a mountain desert
like the shape of smoke from far away.
This is why the dead must be burned, brother,

and why some things cannot be undone,
some wiring in the chemical brain
that can never be rewired again
so you are set adrift
in the world of not undoing,
like the la-de-da damaged boy. It means
you reap what you sow.
It means a galaxy of
everything you've ever
done or seen done wrong and
said nothing
trails behind you like the tail of a comet,
all ice and dark debris,
and we think that
something like angels
will come for us in the end,
and carry us away. I love
the lie that god is; father
forgive me because there is no grace,
only separation, a kind of deviation
from the usual path
but not a wrath you'll ever grasp
even when you see it happen
right before your eyes; I assure you,
only peaceful thoughts, discerning,
yet still there's something inside burning
and I'm on a ride with the hallelujah science.

IV

We don't know how someone could kill that way,
the children in their classrooms safe at school.
Our world is named guns, and bullets spray
free as our American minds are to fool
ourselves that we are good; there's nothing left to do.
Dead children wait in their classrooms
for their mothers and fathers to view

their small bodies; the doom
it is to see your child dead and blue as frozen snow;
you'll never be the same again; you'll never see
the world in gracious light; you'll never know
the quiet peace of simply how to be.
We want to give our lives to bring them back
although I know how foolish sacrifice may sound;
words can say but words can never be,
or stop the bullets, not even a single round
from cutting through the air, until they almost see
the flesh and bone they blast away.
You have to know the fear of how it feels
before you understand.

V

Immigrants, misfits, ne'er-do-wells for benefits,
Croats, Serbs, Polacks, Slovenians,
it's what we mean
when we say where we're from;
summer, and all we have is each other. Brother
do you know how it feels
to have so much of nothing
that you don't even know?

Don't preach to me, don't teach me any remedies
to restore the dualities
in my brain. I know what to do with my ghosts
once the party is over,
and I know how to set an ambush and some claymores
if the need arises; I'm full of surprises,
I like your horizons so full of hope that was never there,
just dope they gave us to forget and not scare
the good citizens around us who may not be aware
of the damage war does to boys and to girls
hurled so far away from love.

VI

The blade of Eros in the form of a message from the spirit of someone
I had watched cross over but who seems to want to stick around blues;
it goes something like this:

Sometimes I do the right thing, and sometimes I don't,
even at this age and
what the hell is that all about?
Love is a ribbon that cuts,
and I have crossed some fleshy bridges, brother,
that gave way to an endless green fall.
I am still falling, father,
mother of the cool sheets,
so, no need for you to wait for me
at the screen door
in just a poor kitchen light any longer,
a ghost without his hauntings.

What went wrong is not a question you should ask people like me.
What went wrong is the name of a way of being,
an evolution towards the entropic and the nuclear,
a requiem for the bad angels, clogging the highway,
a towering catastrophe of lies; opium dreams
of the jungle green spider,
its legs around my face,
a woman who comes in the dark;
oh space, the dream said, don't worry time.
You can lose track of who you are;
you can say all the old Jesus stuff to yourself in the dark,
but if those black wings have your name on them
you might as well saddle-up
my First Sergeant said more than a few times,
and you may think that this is my news, so
what the fuck,
but I accuse us all of the worst crimes. I love us all
for the worst crimes. There is no pure humanity;
it's a metaphor that doesn't work, a dream without a center

you can't wake from.
I'm not talking about myself
but about the map of our stupid failures,
because I don't know where to turn anymore,
and all I want is to get out of this, once and for all.
All I want is a peaceful mind, and a spirit who
longs to stay close,
and some great arms that wrap around me,
and hold me still for a moment of something
that feels exactly like love,
the long night of disciplined emotion
over, the godliness to the nth degree
a cool mist, drowning us in peace.

Part Three

Making the Conscious Darkness

Dancing to Gypsy
banjo music and vodka,
and circa 1985
was the state of my mind,
Rosalina turning wild
circles just inches from my body.

This was after a long time of being lost
in a post-war haze I tried
to drown and smoke away forever.

Every object in the room
was moving to the music
somehow, to our bodies
swaying in the dark basement
bar, and when I tried to spin

like Rosalina
I could feel the world beg
to move, a great weight of blue
light flashing through dark space so
I felt connected to something,
the way your heart is
connected to your brain;
the way a single strand of memory can save you
from cold and loneliness, even if
you want to die. Be grateful,
the wind says at last.

The Beauty

On Plummer Mountain, West Virginia,
the elder Mr. Plummer sits beside me on a couch
someone had dragged outside to the front porch—oh light
of brilliant ideas—so you can sit there
and stare out at the pasture
that was there
instead of what we call a yard, acres
rolling off as far as we could see,
which wasn't that far
because of the hills that cut
our line of vision,

so the bull
could come and then
could disappear
even before the sun went down,
even before the elder Mr. Plummer
said a single word
for a long stretch of time on the porch,
watching the bull come and then
move across our minds you could say.
You could say that was one of those
times of crossing over,
the way the world telescoped
down into a finely focused
moment of nothing happening at all;
the peace in that, the beauty.

Bodhisattva Blurred by Lilies in the Garden

Let me tell you how the life inside a lie
feels, the immense jungle green
shattered by ambush in the evening.
Let me execute myself in peace, dear
strangers whom I love. The turning wheel
is a kind of lie too, unimaginable
photographs of disasters that shatter
into tiny pieces when you try to pick them up, like history.
The world doesn't end or even
notice any of this lush blue orbit
flashing past, let alone my problems, or
yours, the Bodhisattva
blurred by lilies in the garden.

My Araby

"Dear God" I began my letter when I was five years old. I could read and write thanks to my father who never graduated high school but who taught me how to live in the world like a man, how to read a box score and score a game by myself, and how to throw a punch. I was writing to God to save myself from sins I thought so horrible, Christ himself would put an end to my miserable life.

I put my stupid faith in the mailbox on the corner where I'd once frozen my lips to the side, hiding from a police car in the winter night.

There was nothing left but chances by then. The arcade was closing down, its lights blinking off, one by one. Better not to ask why things happen, a waste among some wider wastes; nothing left, except what's left.

Village Parable

When the green begins to go to yellow
you can hear the locust chirp
all through the long evening, the sun
setting just now, the sky
streaked with red,
and every spirit in its place.

I could find a world there. I could find
a way to live inside the village life;
tend my garden, care for my children's
children who play in the dusty courtyard, lose
the last ribbons of myself and be free.

The Love I Thought Would Save Me

No possibility of relief of any kind,
the debris of debris
tumbling haphazard through the metaphysical air;
at least we can put that on the fucking table
so there's no misunderstanding, no possibility of being

there and somewhere else at the same time
is what the doubters say. They say a lot of things
to discount the world layered upon ours
almost invisibly
as spider threads off limestone creek beds,
as glory, which is alright with me.

C, F, AND G

I laughed when she said it was *only* a dream because
she hadn't been with me on that
particular hell ride through some not so recent
events between the sheets that were perfectly
tangled up in blood. She said
it was *just* my imagination,
as if that was not enough
and I did not realize the momentum I had gained
would become such an unstoppable force
towards its beautiful ending: the fireworks,
the chants of monks, the rock and roll,
all suspended in my mind in a single
moment of an otherwise uneventful morning.
The great machinery of stars
shifts in the black sky, but I know it's only
my brain again, trying to heal itself,
three chords
and the words of heaven,
all you need of love.

Modern Paradox Sutra Fragment

A sex offender father broke the jaw
of his four-year-old cerebral
palsy son in an unspecified act
of rage. Change yourself the teacher tells me
again, and again because you can't change anyone else.
Knowing things ensures heartbreak. Not knowing
is worse. Change yourself the teacher says;
make more room for the suffering of others
is what he means. Make more room and then let it
flow through you. Let the broken-jawed little
palsied boy who couldn't even understand
his own poor life flow through you, and let his
blurred screams flow through you and not through you
to feel them deeply and then to let them go.

Moon Sutra

You can't fool me you flesh-eating moon. I've bared
myself to your light more than a few good
times and felt a jarring jolt of something—
moon, or what pulls the moon, or what the moon
pulls to slow itself down—and then I said
is that all you get for your fucking money.

Love in Space

The two maples are dying but
they won't admit it so no,
the bare winter branches don't make them
look the same as every other tree.
When we turn towards winter
there is a particular gray light that comes
to inhabit the late afternoons and
evenings. It may or may not be
dangerous to be caught in that light.
It happened to me once,
I was transported by some eyes
so far away I could barely hold on.
If you resist, you're pulled further in.
Watch the miles disappear, watch the time
mean nothing,
watch the love grow and tangle, and then grow again.

The Sixty-sixth Year of My Imagining

The frozen air comes early to the year,
surprising everyone with blinding snow,
the leaves still in the trees, where ghosts appear
and rattle in the branches beyond hope.
Some birds are trapped, they don't know how to leave
now that the landscape has completely changed;
it isn't that they feel that they should grieve
but more that things are suddenly deranged.
How many times can we be fooled when
every year it is the same, the light
pulls back so dark can take its place, pretending
everything will be alright.
Inside the coldest night our sleep is warm,
that's how we finally die inside the storm.

For Night

I don't think it's my place to breathe, Mr. Night.
I don't think it's my place to say any fucking
howdy-do to anyone in this polite
asylum of a world, not any more,
not after everything that's happened to you
and to me. There used to be a silence
you could count on, like a thick rope dropped

down from heaven, but the voices have come back
from the dead, even if the bodies haven't,
and they fill my head with their last words
which are not always Goodbyes, but sometimes
a plea for more light, or for a forgiveness
impossible to give them. I have known you more
than once in foreign dark, where you finally
spoke to me, your code a shiver
through my body, showing me the way,
and you were never wrong as long
as I gave myself to you completely,
utterly, in the rarefied jungle air,
oh night who still attends me like a worried
mother, or like a lover with a cause, don't you see.

Dismantling Bruce Weigl at Gate Number 7

I was plotting a tasteful escape
from a gathering of men
(I wrote "snakes" at first)
I'd found myself somehow
tangled among in a small room
I had followed a misunderstanding to;
through some alleyways,
across from Lenin Park I was,
"Joy to the fishes in the deep blue sea"
strangely on someone's radio;
I counted the bodies of men
around me in the dark. I hardly
barely bowed and smiled as if
I was angry. Through the only door
my eyes found a way in the dark
but I waited for what would happen
next, unafraid of death or of
anything else, a tic in my neuro-pathways,
an addiction always to what's next
as if the moment didn't matter.
Two men carried in a heavy urn
covered with Chinese characters,
sealed with wax and a bright red cloth,
another man brought in a tray,
a small white cup for each of us,
and I watched the door and all other
possible openings unhinge themselves.
What happens next is nothing we
should speak of indelicately,
ancient eyes or not through the curtains
that were not curtains at all,
I recall, now, back at the gate,
exactly one thousand years
after it was raised, in defiance.

My Father's Money

No mathematician, still,
I knew my fractions and shined
in class that term with answers.
When you're poor you learn the fractions
early, how half of nothing
is somehow even less,
how to cut the hungry times
into slices of forgetting,
and the long nights into dreams
not fractured by the wild family life.
I asked my father once,
in nineteen fifty something,
for three lousy dollars
to buy some baseball spikes
from a kid down the block.
I know now what I didn't know then,
that when he said he didn't have the money,
he meant it, and that three dollars
was a lot in our house,
poor as cabbage soup,
but all of us close together
near the coal stove in the dark,
near the coal stove, in the dark.

A Mishap

The blank of blank
the science of dying
the black cat changing rooms
caught for a moment
in some brilliant sun
the pathology of fear
one LA car
slamming into another
is not like slow motion
and some lost things
can never be recovered but
thank Ra for the light
that let us see so clearly
the unreal aftermath
thank the kind Egyptian man
who owned a garage nearby
witness to the collision
who helped me to his limousine
then delivered me
to the door of salvation by air
the everything I don't remember
the desert wind
dry as a breath
in the battle of love
night flight
shock tight now shoulders and neck
and an uneasy dreaminess
come over me like warm waves
of whatever it is that keeps changing
from black to white inside my brain
Cleveland two a.m.
sick and dizzy at the VA
like a drunk or a junkie nodding
my brain a whirr

of unidentifiable pictures
of a background from someone else's life.
What is this, I ask the light,
and the light blasts down on me
something I could feel through my spine
and through my groin,
a sharp chain pulled through me
then something flying out of my body
Oh thing
flying out of my body
I don't worship you
I worship no man or woman or no god or myth or story
I have stood in a sunlit green valley
filled with hidden terrors and sudden death
yet lost myself
in the way through leaves and branches
the light spears rained down sometimes
or maybe that's my rattled brain
because I don't remember everything
the crash a wild blur and boom three times
like mortar rounds
the way that they come down
so you can hear them
is where my brain was sent
in one hard second of contact
metal on plastic on metal
the force at fifty MPH
like a storm inside your skull and neck
that whipped me
I don't know what it is that stays with me
I escaped some paperwork and the cops
and left the scene
there on the corner of Lincoln Blvd
the Mexican woman thanking Jesus,
her praying hands in the air like black birds,
the stunned driver unable to comprehend the loss,
the Egyptian man, who read my eyes somehow

and got me out of there,
a circle I keep finding
when I try to find my way.

Sweeping in the Temple

The infidelity of granite
blocks they laid two thousand years ago is
of particular interest to the
locals, and nothing was enough to feed
the machine in those days. Nothing meant
nothing, and the wind said not a single
word, even in the tree limbs' bare existence.

The other side of the story would be
different of course. This is just something
to let roll through you, and then to let go.
Centuries have passed since I began here.

What If I Told You

that the sky was such a perfect pale blue
of an Easter egg or of
the beginnings of a bruise
around the eyes
that it would not release me
to my worldly duties. Meanwhile
the Chinese elm calls
its evening birds into their places
high in the leafy branches
where things are safe for now.
All afternoon long I wait, drowsing,
for the cardinals to return
who finally arrive together,
and make a kind of sense
that rocks you back.
Still, if you add it all up
it comes to zero; forget
the billion plus stars;
when their light reaches you
they are already dead.

Oh Denial

See how it goes
all around the roses
what I had in mind
never mind
the red wing black bird
I murdered
said to the wind
who did not care

So solitary in our own madness
that even an encore
couldn't keep us
from leaving the burning theater
the mass not yet at its liturgy
Oh psychedelic
to coin a phrase
Oh, so American the denial
the tenderness of our escapes
from the hardened
light-reflecting real
world, if only for a moment.

For a Friend Whose Son Is in Prison

What do you do with the guilty, when they are one of your own? What do you do with a son whose one bad judgment cost him so much time? Only love will do in such cases; anything else pales in the face of such tragedy.

How well we know words and look what it's gotten us. How well we know the lie of words that can make a good thing happen, just when you need it, and then mean nothing at all.

When you told me about your long drive on visitor's day, I could see you so clearly that I was

stunned, riding there beside you for a moment, and I could feel the weight of your sadness like a barge, trapped in dark water, going nowhere but in circles, to the bottom.

Not an Elegy for F.

The wounded cardinal chick, caught out in the open,
the frantic parents darting in and out as if to illustrate some
        pattern
that seems too complicated.
It doesn't help,
                        and all the racket has called the cats,
whom I love and had named after my grandfather
and his sweet brother from the old country. Don't say
                                                                There was
        nothing I could do, or, That's nature.
                                                Don't say
                                                                Holes in the sky
instead of stars above your grave. Say Holes in the sky, instead of stars, above your grave.

Blue Late Elegy for R.

When my dead friend comes to visit me, I am grateful, and I say so. He reminds me of the beautifully crazy things we did together over our fifty-five years, all the wonderful, wasted time, and I don't know why he must always leave so quickly, as if something called him or pulled him back into that other—what is it—realm? but while he is here, I can feel him like the brother that he is to me, and smell the scent of him strong as all of memory, and hear the river of his voice not exactly call to me, but say something that only makes sense deep in our lives together, a confirmation that it's him, like the stone I keep in my pocket for those times when I don't know where I am. The stone is always in the world. The wheel turns and new graves are dug, new houses built. The wheel turns and someone else is gone and no matter how many times these wisps of him come into my room to sit with me and smoke, he is still gone so long without the living touch from those who no longer wait. They no longer wait for him.

The Clock on the Tower in Hà Nội

It wasn't a question of romance
but more a sudden thunder storm
with rain so heavy we were all driven
from our chairs outside the café
and then crowded together
inside the small shop, waiting
for the rain to stop. A woman
sat on the counter, and some boys
and small girls already napped on their mothers' laps.
There was no panic or agitation;
there was some talk about the weather,
and how strange it had been,
and when the rain slowed but didn't stop
I stepped outside to see the sky.
It was a practical matter
when the woman lifted her umbrella
and stood on her toes to reach
above my head to keep me dry.
I thanked her, and asked if I could hold the umbrella
and she nodded and smiled. Oh
I held it there until the rain stopped,

and our eyes on the other's eyes
took us somewhere else for a moment,
drawn out like specks of dust in sunlight.
I pulled it closed and shook the water off
before I handed it back to her. In Vietnamese
I thanked her, and I bowed. In Vietnamese
she said that I was welcome and we
both had somewhere else to go
so turned away into our only crowd, day
beating like a drum, like the clock
on a tower in Hà Nội.

Mr. O.'s Peach Tree

The peach tree's all but one blossom
killed by a late frost
so there will only be one peach
that I wish for someone else's mouth,
the she of the years,
to suckle the sweet juice
and then kiss me long and slow
because we have only our moments,
and I think the trees will remember me
although it's a problem
of the amygdala
as it turns out,
a switch turned on and then broken,
so fear leaks in. There is no sense
to wish it hadn't. You step into each new
moment of your life
as if you knew where you were going,
and the annoying sun,
without which we would be dead,
floods the speeding car you ride in
towards salvation, a single peach blossom
that survived a late frost
and went on with its peachy life.

Her Discontent like Lava Soap Burns in the Eyes

Who do you go to   Oh la

She resisted the fire
an ABC of loneliness

Part of the sun fell into her head

At the batting cage
cadence is everything
cadence is birdsong harmony

Bless this hall of fame
or else there's no more river water sit downs

We fail in the blood
is where it fucking happens.

Part of the sun fell into her head.

A Small Song for Immigrants

The immigrants ride bicycles through town.
They blend in now and mostly work behind the scenes
for wages most Americans would never take,
and think they live in paradise. How bad
it must have been to have to run away
from home and family, the poor lined up

along the dust clogged road to nowhere,
their hands held out to passing motorcars
as if someone could help. No one can help
you from the damage to your soul that being
hungry means, that living under bloody rule,
not free to even say the names of someone dead.
The immigrants ride bicycles through town.
They blend in now and mostly work behind the scenes.

The Failure of Cognitive Therapy on April 26, 2015

Well, I can bless myself
it just this moment occurred to me
as a passenger
in a partly angry car
zooming towards errands
of a nature unknown to me.
"Bless you" I can say
and the pronoun's reference
is me, the blessing
no less shining.

Isn't this life luscious
and so distant at the same time
so that you never know
how much to take,
or how hard
to press yourself
against the wire boundary
of all of memory;
no thank you Dr. X,
I think I'll pass on certain details,
and let the fragments of memory
continue to have their morbid,
their unorderly charming way with me,
and burst through my head
like tracer rounds
in a moment otherwise given
to peaceful work or quiet meditation.
I know how well you mean,
your compassion
a rising tide of warm water around me,
but you weren't there.
You don't know how we felt.

Kill everything
they told us, kill them all.

For Steven, Boone School, 1956

The visitors keep coming to the park,
there isn't anything for them to do
but mull around, inquiring where the body
was, after he was done with her.
There's some who knew her from the neighborhood,
the rest are strangers satisfying some other
need, a taste for blood that even pounding
rain can't quite erase, its shadow stained
across the pavement near the swings where children
play; the first to find the body
only six years old, forget the damage
done to him. I knew him in the early
grades; he never seemed the same again,
as if some light was squashed inside
so darkness flooded in. The lives of children
flash so quickly past our knowing
it's all that we can do
to have a moment here and there,
and I wonder how the boy who found the body
turned out, what kind of man he is,
and if he ever grew out of the silence
that had surrounded him from that day forward.
I sat behind him in class. He never said a word again,
and sat alone at recess and at lunch,
but now he's grown, he's old like me,
and if we hear the same bells jangled,
it only means it's time for us to leave.

Song of H.

Why do we murder ourselves
and then try to live forever.
At the exact heart of
Shenandoah, Miami,
a peacock crosses the busy street
unconcerned with cars and trucks
who stop or slow down;
one large feather has lost its color
and drags behind
like a bad memory
is where I find myself
because I can never fully
escape the war
and the wars today and tomorrow,
because forty years later
I can close my eyes
and still see what hot metal
does to human flesh,
the someone who died in our arms
for example, or the traffic here
that moves faster and faster
until it's a blur of noisy color,
a perfectly horizontal rainbow
that you can follow
block to block to your bliss,
unless you murder yourself first,
or try to live forever
like you were a star or something,
a galaxy unto yourself,
all the poor soldiers
who didn't come home
barely balanced on my back.
I try to swim them home
on a night river named Cà Lu,

but it's burdened with ambush
so we are driven back to the trees
of our awakening,
but no one says the word
die, although that's what I felt
and I would have given anything,
done anything, robbed or lied, said anything
for one more breathe of jungle air that night,
like the prick of the needle
as it makes a hole
so you can live again.

Kokura Bar

The bar maid flirts with older men,
veterans of a bitter war;
a few drinks
and everything seems okay,
a few lies and
what's the harm in that?
She makes them smile,
that temporary state of flux
desire brings,
and then something
unexpected
happens in the name of salvation.
Oh, I heard the shots fired,
but my body took me to the floor
until the firing stopped. Flash
and I'm right back home again,
that's how easy it is to get my attention. Flash
and how quickly everything
collapses into a white hole of
what you need to do to stay alive. This
I am guilty of, and I'm sorry if I
frightened you
or if I made you worry that
aching worry grief brings, but
there was nothing I could do.
One small trigger you see,
and I'm all lit up.

Thinking About the Chinese Poet

Beautiful half moon
beyond clouds that don't move
except the way
everything moves
away from us,
so I wonder what the
Chinese poet would write,
what he would want to say
against so much darkness,

a black sea seeping in.

I wonder if the Chinese poet
would think it was wise
to open one's self up like this
to the darkness
and invite the darkness in
like a stranger, on a rainy night.

I think he had a different kind of worry—
to get his small boat
home before dark,
to find his flower
waiting for him,
hiding in the rushes
behind her silk fan,
and to thank the river
and the spirits who gather there
in the half moon, beyond clouds.

My When I Have Fears

Kingdom of loneliness in the
bright sun and cool
mountain air. No human
voices sometimes for days,
the blowing rock
nearly visible through the thinning trees
and the blue expanse of sky,
and you have to be somewhere
at all times is the rule, or you'll have trouble,
and be out of sync with the good citizens
who keep the faith
however just under the surface
where the purely human rage
lingers too, like a wisp of something
wrong in the air, or in the stuttering speech of strangers
whom you wish were in a dream. Look around the room
the Dr. reminds me, to remember where I am,
and sometimes this helps
to reel me back from what I cannot allow myself
to remember. Do you know that fear?
I dream of an emptiness that calls me
but no sirens' call back from the rocks
and instead, a faithful wooing towards grace;
imagine you're looking over my shoulder.
Imagine you're right here
watching me write this down
against all odds
and in the name of beautiful
spirits who never come
except in cups of light you drink from
in the garden, voices all around you
a rushing herd,
so you relinquish,
you let go of everything and fly apart

into atoms of whatever it is
that binds us,
that makes us feel this way.

Crazy with His Anguish and Dumb with Grief

The air above the moving water.
The air above the moving water.
Cool spring air above the moving water.
The river comes from where it goes.
Stand in the deeply moving river long enough
and you can feel what time is, and what time is not.
You can be jolted from one way of seeing
into a wholly other way of strangers crossing over
who don't belong among us,
a conspiracy of the dead you could call them.
You could call them a shroud that moves through the room
like a tiny black cloud and then disappears,
although stranger things have happened.

The air above the moving water is
cool in spring. I believe in a paradise of words,
like the words you find under great rocks in the river,
and the words high in the branches on night wind,
and the words that tell a secret kept for so long
it can never be forgiven. I believe
in the leaves turning up, before the storm
is even in our sight. In a vacuum
there is no sorrow or longing. Everything
they taught us was about living, with nothing
about how to die. The air above
the moving water is cool in the spring.
The wheel turns, and you're back again
to the same place. The less time you have,
the more beautiful everything in the world appears.

Acknowledgments

I offer my grateful acknowledgment for the support of editors of magazines in which these poems first appeared:

American Poetry Review: "The Hà Nội Winds Bringing Winter to the Old-World Elegy," "Lotus, West Lake, 2010," "Lotus," "The Elephant Gift in the Room," "For Night," and "Crazy with His Anguish and Dumb with Grief";
Cold Mountain Review: "On the Shores of Welcome Home," "The World Part II," and "The Sixty-sixth Year of My Imagining";
Connotation Press: An On-line Artifact: "Bodhisattva Blurred by Lilies in the Garden," "For Night," "What If I Told You," "The Clock on the Tower in Hà Nội," "A Small Song for Immigrants";
Great River Review: "The Beauty" and "The World Part II";
Irish Literary Times: "Grace Being Saved";
Meat for Tea: The Valley Review: "Love in Space";
Miramar: "Against Poetry," "Fragments in Translation from the Vietnamese," "Modern Paradox Sutra Fragment," "Village Parable," and "The Love I Thought Would Save Me";
Pedestal: "A Mishap" and "Song of H.";
The Rattling Wall: "Anecdote of the Impresario of My Brain," "Some Stages of the Mayfly," and "River of Blood in One Man";
Teaching English in the Two-Year College: "The Long-Term Consequences of the Convoy Leading to Pegasus in the Fallen World" and "A Late Corrupted Flash."

"Lotus" also appeared as a North River Books Broadside under its Vietnamese title, "Hoa Sen." Thanks to Ray Amorossi.

I am also grateful to the Lannan Foundation and the Lannan family for their enduring support of my artistic life. Thanks to Reg Gibbons, Kevin Bowen, Nguyễn Bá Chung, Carolyn Forché, Robert Hass, Nguyễn Quang Thiều, Nguyễn Pham Quế Mai, and Xia Lu for their support and their friendship. Thanks finally to my editor Peter Conners for his great eye, and for his true support, and to the staff at BOA Editions, Ltd., for their remarkable professionalism and gentle kindness.

Dedications:

"Prayer for My Teacher" is for Nguyễn Bá Chung.

"Fragments in Translation from the Vietnamese" is for Trung Trung Đỉnh.

"On the Shores of Welcome Home" is for Yusef, with gratitude for his poems.

"The Beauty" is for Claudio, whose art inspires me.

"For Night" is for Charles Simic, my teacher.

"Dismantling Bruce Weigl at Gate Number 7" is for Hua Thỉnh, with gratitude for his friendship and support.

"Mishap" is for Shelley, in memorial.

"Oh Denial" is for K.C.

"Her Discontent like Lava Soap Burns in the Eyes" is for J. T., in memorial.

"Thinking of the Chinese Poet" is for Xia Lu.

About the Author

Bruce Weigl previously published *The Abundance of Nothing* (TriQuarterly Books), one of three finalists for the Pulitzer Prize in Poetry in 2013, a memoir—*The Circle of Hạnh* (Grove Press, 2000)— as well as more than twenty-five other works of poetry, essays, and translations from the Vietnamese and the Romanian. He lives in Oberlin, Ohio, and in Hà Nội, Việt Nam where he reads, writes, and translates.

BOA Editions, Ltd., American Poets Continuum Series

No. 1 *The Fuhrer Bunker: A Cycle of Poems in Progress*
W. D. Snodgrass

No. 2 *She*
M. L. Rosenthal

No. 3 *Living With Distance*
Ralph J. Mills, Jr.

No. 4 *Not Just Any Death*
Michael Waters

No. 5 *That Was Then: New and Selected Poems*
Isabella Gardner

No. 6 *Things That Happen Where There Aren't Any People*
William Stafford

No. 7 *The Bridge of Change: Poems 1974–1980*
John Logan

No. 8 *Signatures*
Joseph Stroud

No. 9 *People Live Here: Selected Poems 1949–1983*
Louis Simpson

No. 10 *Yin*
Carolyn Kizer

No. 11 *Duhamel: Ideas of Order in Little Canada*
Bill Tremblay

No. 12 *Seeing It Was So*
Anthony Piccione

No. 13 *Hyam Plutzik: The Collected Poems*

No. 14 *Good Woman: Poems and a Memoir 1969–1980*
Lucille Clifton

No. 15 *Next: New Poems*
Lucille Clifton

No. 16 *Roxa: Voices of the Culver Family*
William B. Patrick

No. 17 *John Logan: The Collected Poems*

No. 18 *Isabella Gardner: The Collected Poems*

No. 19 *The Sunken Lightship*
Peter Makuck

No. 20 *The City in Which I Love You*
Li-Young Lee

No. 21 *Quilting: Poems 1987–1990*
Lucille Clifton

No. 22 *John Logan: The Collected Fiction*

No. 23 *Shenandoah and Other Verse Plays*
Delmore Schwartz

No. 24 *Nobody Lives on Arthur Godfrey Boulevard*
Gerald Costanzo

No. 25 *The Book of Names: New and Selected Poems*
Barton Sutter

No. 26 *Each in His Season*
W. D. Snodgrass

No. 27 *Wordworks: Poems Selected and New*
Richard Kostelanetz

No. 28 *What We Carry*
Dorianne Laux

No. 29 *Red Suitcase*
Naomi Shihab Nye

No. 30 *Song*
Brigit Pegeen Kelly

No. 31 *The Fuehrer Bunker: The Complete Cycle*
W. D. Snodgrass

No. 32 *For the Kingdom*
Anthony Piccione

No. 33 *The Quicken Tree*
Bill Knott

No. 34 *These Upraised Hands*
William B. Patrick

No. 35 *Crazy Horse in Stillness*
William Heyen

No. 36 *Quick, Now, Always*
Mark Irwin

No. 37 *I Have Tasted the Apple*
Mary Crow

No. 38 *The Terrible Stories*
Lucille Clifton

No. 39 *The Heat of Arrivals*
Ray Gonzalez

No. 40 *Jimmy & Rita*
Kim Addonizio

No. 41 *Green Ash, Red Maple, Black Gum*
Michael Waters

No. 42 *Against Distance*
Peter Makuck

No. 43 *The Night Path*
Laurie Kutchins

No. 44 *Radiography*
Bruce Bond

No. 45 *At My Ease: Uncollected Poems of the Fifties and Sixties*
David Ignatow

No. 46 *Trillium*
Richard Foerster

No. 47 *Fuel*
Naomi Shihab Nye

No. 48 *Gratitude*
Sam Hamill

No. 49 *Diana, Charles, & the Queen*
William Heyen

No. 50 *Plus Shipping*
Bob Hicok

No. 51 *Cabato Sentora*
Ray Gonzalez

No. 52 *We Didn't Come Here for This*
William B. Patrick

No. 53 *The Vandals*
Alan Michael Parker

No. 54 *To Get Here*
Wendy Mnookin

No. 55 *Living Is What I Wanted: Last Poems*
David Ignatow

No. 56 *Dusty Angel*
Michael Blumenthal

No. 57 *The Tiger Iris*
Joan Swift

No. 58 *White City*
Mark Irwin

No. 59 *Laugh at the End of the World: Collected Comic Poems 1969–1999*
Bill Knott

No. 60 *Blessing the Boats: New and Selected Poems: 1988–2000*
Lucille Clifton

No. 61 *Tell Me*
Kim Addonizio

No. 62 *Smoke*
Dorianne Laux

No. 63 *Parthenopi: New and Selected Poems*
Michael Waters

No. 64 *Rancho Notorious*
Richard Garcia

No. 65 *Jam*
Joe-Anne McLaughlin

No. 66 *A. Poulin, Jr. Selected Poems*
Edited, with an Introduction by Michael Waters

No. 67 *Small Gods of Grief*
Laure-Anne Bosselaar

No. 68 *Book of My Nights*
Li-Young Lee

No. 69 *Tulip Farms and Leper Colonies*
Charles Harper Webb

No. 70 *Double Going*
Richard Foerster

No. 71 *What He Took*
Wendy Mnookin

No. 72 *The Hawk Temple at Tierra Grande*
Ray Gonzalez

No. 73 *Mules of Love*
Ellen Bass

No. 74 *The Guests at the Gate*
Anthony Piccione

No. 75 *Dumb Luck*
Sam Hamill

No. 76 *Love Song with Motor Vehicles*
Alan Michael Parker

No. 77 *Life Watch*
Willis Barnstone

No. 78 *The Owner of the House: New Collected Poems 1940–2001*
Louis Simpson

No. 79 *Is*
Wayne Dodd

No. 80 *Late*
Cecilia Woloch

No. 81 *Precipitates*
Debra Kang Dean

No. 82 *The Orchard*
Brigit Pegeen Kelly

No. 83 *Bright Hunger*
Mark Irwin

No. 84 *Desire Lines: New and Selected Poems*
Lola Haskins

No. 85 *Curious Conduct*
Jeanne Marie Beaumont

No. 86 *Mercy*
Lucille Clifton

No. 87 *Model Homes*
Wayne Koestenbaum

No. 88 *Farewell to the Starlight in Whiskey*
Barton Sutter

No. 89 *Angels for the Burning*
David Mura

No. 90 *The Rooster's Wife*
Russell Edson

No. 91 *American Children*
Jim Simmerman

No. 92 *Postcards from the Interior*
Wyn Cooper

No. 93 *You & Yours*
Naomi Shihab Nye

No. 94 *Consideration of the Guitar: New and Selected Poems 1986–2005*
Ray Gonzalez

No. 95 *Off-Season in the Promised Land*
Peter Makuck

No. 96 *The Hoopoe's Crown*
Jacqueline Osherow

No. 97 *Not for Specialists: New and Selected Poems*
W. D. Snodgrass

No. 98 *Splendor*
Steve Kronen

No. 99 *Woman Crossing a Field*
Deena Linett

No. 100 *The Burning of Troy*
Richard Foerster

No. 101 *Darling Vulgarity*
Michael Waters

No. 102 *The Persistence of Objects*
Richard Garcia

No. 103 *Slope of the Child Everlasting*
Laurie Kutchins

No. 104 *Broken Hallelujahs*
Sean Thomas Dougherty

No. 105 *Peeping Tom's Cabin: Comic Verse 1928–2008*
X. J. Kennedy

No. 106 *Disclamor*
G.C. Waldrep

No. 107 *Encouragement for a Man Falling to His Death*
Christopher Kennedy

No. 108 *Sleeping with Houdini*
Nin Andrews

No. 109 *Nomina*
Karen Volkman

No. 110 *The Fortieth Day*
Kazim Ali

No. 111 *Elephants & Butterflies*
Alan Michael Parker

No. 112 *Voices*
Lucille Clifton

No. 113 *The Moon Makes Its Own Plea*
Wendy Mnookin

No. 114 *The Heaven-Sent Leaf*
Katy Lederer

No. 115 *Struggling Times*
Louis Simpson

No. 116 *And*
Michael Blumenthal

No. 117 *Carpathia*
Cecilia Woloch

No. 118 *Seasons of Lotus, Seasons of Bone*
Matthew Shenoda

No. 119 *Sharp Stars*
Sharon Bryan

No. 120 *Cool Auditor*
Ray Gonzalez

No. 121 *Long Lens: New and Selected Poems*
Peter Makuck

No. 122 *Chaos Is the New Calm*
Wyn Cooper

No. 123 *Diwata*
Barbara Jane Reyes

No. 124 *Burning of the Three Fires*
Jeanne Marie Beaumont

No. 125 *Sasha Sings the Laundry on the Line*
Sean Thomas Dougherty

No. 126 *Your Father on the Train of Ghosts*
G.C. Waldrep and John Gallaher

No. 127 *Ennui Prophet*
Christopher Kennedy

No. 128 *Transfer*
Naomi Shihab Nye

No. 129 *Gospel Night*
Michael Waters

No. 130 *The Hands of Strangers: Poems from the Nursing Home*
Janice N. Harrington

No. 131 *Kingdom Animalia*
Aracelis Girmay

No. 132 *True Faith*
Ira Sadoff

No. 133 *The Reindeer Camps and Other Poems*
Barton Sutter

No. 134 *The Collected Poems of Lucille Clifton: 1965–2010*

No. 135 *To Keep Love Blurry*
Craig Morgan Teicher

No. 136 *Theophobia*
Bruce Beasley

No. 137 *Refuge*
Adrie Kusserow

No. 138 *The Book of Goodbyes*
Jillian Weise

No. 139 *Birth Marks*
Jim Daniels

No. 140 *No Need of Sympathy*
Fleda Brown

No. 141 *There's a Box in the Garage You Can Beat with a Stick*
Michael Teig

No. 142 *The Keys to the Jail*
Keetje Kuipers

No. 143 *All You Ask for Is Longing: New and Selected Poems 1994–2014*
Sean Thomas Dougherty

No. 144 *Copia*
Erika Meitner

No. 145 *The Chair: Prose Poems*
Richard Garcia

No. 146 *In a Landscape*
John Gallaher

No. 147 *Fanny Says*
Nickole Brown

No. 148 *Why God Is a Woman*
Nin Andrews

No. 149 *Testament*
G.C. Waldrep

No. 150 *I'm No Longer Troubled by the Extravagance*
Rick Bursky

No. 151 *Antidote for Night*
Marsha de la O

No. 152 *Beautiful Wall*
Ray Gonzalez

No. 153 *the black maria*
Aracelis Girmay

No. 154 *Celestial Joyride*
Michael Waters

No. 155 *Whereso*
Karen Volkman

No. 156 *The Day's Last Light Reddens the Leaves of the Copper Beech*
Stephen Dobyns

No. 157 *The End of Pink*
Kathryn Nuernberger

No. 158 *Mandatory Evacuation*
Peter Makuck

No. 159 *Primitive: The Art and Life of Horace H. Pippin*
Janice N. Harrington

No. 160 *The Trembling Answers*
Craig Morgan Teicher

No. 161 *Bye-Bye Land*
Christian Barter

No. 162 *Sky Country*
Christine Kitano

No. 163 *All Soul Parts Returned*
Bruce Beasley

No. 164 *The Smoke of Horses*
Charles Rafferty

No. 165 *The Second O of Sorrow*
Sean Thomas Dougherty

No. 166 *Holy Moly Carry Me*
Erika Meitner

No. 167 *Clues from the Animal Kingdom*
Christopher Kennedy

No. 168 *Dresses from the Old Country*
Laura Read

No. 169 *In Country*
Hugh Martin

No. 170 *The Tiny Journalist*
Naomi Shihab Nye

No. 171 *All Its Charms*
Keetje Kuipers

No. 172 *Night Angler*
Geffrey Davis

No. 173 *The Human Half*
Deborah Brown

No. 174 *Cyborg Detective*
Jillian Weise

No. 175 *On the Shores of Welcome Home*
Bruce Weigl

Colophon

The Isabella Gardner Poetry Award is given biennially to a poet in mid-career with a new book of exceptional merit. Poet, actress, and associate editor of *Poetry* magazine, Isabella Gardner (1915–1981) published five celebrated collections of poetry, was three times nominated for the National Book Award, and was the first recipient of the New York State Walt Whitman Citation of Merit for Poetry. She championed the work of young and gifted poets, helping many of them to find publication.

The publication of this book is made possible, in part,
by the support of the following individuals:

Anonymous
Rick Bursky
Gary & Gwen Conners
Don Fox, *in honor of my comrades*
at Armed Forces Vietnam Radio Network (AFVN)
James Long Hale
Art & Pam Hatton
Sandi Henschel, *in loving memory of Robert Keesey*
Adrie Kusserow, *in honor of Bruce Weigl*
Jack & Gail Langerak
Joe McElveney
Dan Meyers, *in honor of J. Shepard Skiff*
Wendy & Jim Mnookin
Boo Poulin
Deborah Ronnen
Steven O. Russell & Phyllis Rifkin-Russell
William Waddell & Linda Rubel
Michael Waters & Mihaela Moscaliuc